10TH ANNIVERSARY EDITION

THEY CALLED ME 299-359

POETRY BY THE
INCARCERATED YOUTH OF FREE MINDS

FOREWORD BY
REGINALD DWAYNE BETTS

BOOK CLUB & WRITING WORKSHOP
Empowering young inmates to write new chapters in their lives.

Free Minds Editorial Team
Tara Libert, Managing Editor
Kelli Taylor, Project Editor
Juliana Ratner, Project Editor
Kenneth, Editor and Free Minds Poet
Paulo, Editor and Free Minds Poet
Jonas, Editor and Free Minds Poet

Free Minds Book Club & Writing Workshop is a DC-based nonprofit organization that uses the literary arts, workforce development, and violence prevention to connect incarcerated and formerly incarcerated youths and adults to their voices, their purpose, and the wider community.

Shout Mouse Press is a nonprofit writing and publishing program dedicated to amplifying underheard voices. Learn more and see our full catalog at www.shoutmousepress.org

Shout Mouse Press, 1638 R Street NW Suite 218, Washington, DC 20009
Trade distribution: Ingram Publisher Services International
For information about special discounts and bulk purchases, please contact Shout Mouse Press sales at 240-772-1545 or orders@shoutmousepress.org.

Dedicated to all Free Minds members who use
writing to teach, to heal, to build communities, and
to transform lives and change systems.

And to our Free Minds members whose lives have been lost:

*James, Cortez, Derrick,
Christian, JohnQuan, Nadar, Andre,
Darond, Dontel, Tyree, Antwone,
Amari, Kuron, Dwayne, Darnell,
Marcus, Wayne, Eric, Sharod, Arthur,
Isaiah, DeMario, Mshairi, Tahlil,
Joshua, John, Delonte, Eddie,
Gary, Benny, Michael, David*

And finally, to the original Free Mind:

Glen

CONTENTS

Chapter 1
My World, *By Jonas*
Birthplace, *By William aka Prince Rich*
The Day of My Mother's Death, *By CW*
My Life Story, *By Nick*
I Come From…, *By Anonymous*
De Donde Vengo, *Por Luís*
Where I Come From, *By Luís*

Chapter 2
Unknown Victim, *By Nick*
Hard Times, *By DeVonte*
I Never Thought I'd Be A Hero, *By John*
I Remember, *By Derrick*
The Very Long Journey, *By Oscar*
A Sight I Will Always Remember, *By Alvin*
The Perfect Child, *By Delonte*
Young Forever, *By SN*

Contents

Contents

Contents

ACKNOWLEDGMENTS

We are grateful for the generosity of both individuals and institutions that make our work possible. Free Minds receives and has received financial support from the following:

Clark-Winchcole Foundation
Crowell & Moring Foundation
DC Commission on the Arts and Humanities
DC Office of Victim Services and Justice Grants
Elkes Foundation
Eugene and Agnes E. Meyer Foundation
Greater Washington Community Foundation
Harman Family Foundation
The Herb Block Foundation
The Humanities Council of Washington, DC
The International Monetary Fund
John Edward Fowler Memorial Foundation
Lainoff Family Foundation
Mid-Atlantic Arts Foundation
Miller & Chevalier Charitable Foundation
Miller-Wehrle Family Foundation
Morris & Gwendolyn Cafritz Foundation
Philip L. Graham Fund
Public Welfare Foundation
Rossetter Foundation
Rotary Foundation of Washington, DC
Share Fund
The SuPau Trust Private Foundation
Takoma Foundation

This book was funded in part through a grant from the Capitol Hill Community Foundation.

Free Minds thanks the DC Department of Corrections for their steadfast commitment to our program. We are also grateful for the support of the Correctional Treatment Facility and all staff and teachers of DCPS Incarcerated Youth Program.

FOREWORD

My name is my name, says Marlo, in a memorable moment of David Simon's classic HBO series *The Wire*. Your name, what you're called, what you demand to be called. For many of us, those names include nicknames, include people calling us by our last names, include the names we've chosen. Men and women and children—and children—who have had handcuffs and sentences in detention centers and prisons. For us, we get called numbers. I still remember mine. The writers in the book, they remember theirs. And the first edition of this book, the title meant to point that out. *They Call Me 299-359.*

Things have changed though. Not just have some of the members of Free Minds found their freedom. But even inside, amongst us all, there is this notion that we have ownership over our names. My name is my name. But I won't forget, we won't forget, what they called us. And so, you're holding *They* Called *Me 299-359.* Because you shouldn't forget either.

When the last edition of this book was printed, Michael, one of the poets in this book, was free. And now, he has made his way back into a prison cell. And though his case, like most of ours, ain't about guilt or innocence, the cell that he sits in today is all about what he's been called for so long. It's still a question of what all of us needed, and how what we've been called, how the state number and the cells made it harder and harder for us to become what we might be. What I know though is that writing is the invention of the self, the discovery of the self, and the demand that our identities, that the very essence of who we are, not be confined to a sequence of numbers.

I left prison and fully expected to never return. For my homeboys, I owed money for commissary and letters. But my life, whatever was to happen after those cells, I imagined was all about me. Somewhere along the line, early on, I met Kelli and Tara. And with them, I returned to a jail, for a book club of all things. I was still new enough to prison that anxiety followed me inside (and I'd learn later, with each return to a jail or prison, that the anxiety doesn't leave). I didn't want to wear a name tag. My short locs, denim jeans, and mostly my brown skin led a guard to tell me that the badge they'd given me was all that separated me from the men inside the DC Jail. With the badge on, I walked into a unit filled with young men. All headed for prison. I looked into their eyes and we talked shop: my memoir, other books, poetry. In that room they wrote, and reimagined. And, in that room we all recognized that we are more than whatever violence brought us. Recognized that we are all more because with every syllable we wrote that more into existence.

The thing about Free Minds though is that it is about more than literature. It is about not forgetting. Kelli was partly inspired to start this because of Glen McGinnis, who she'd begun writing after a story she produced on his life. McGinnis was one of the last men executed for a crime committed before their eighteenth birthday. My first year of law school, I carried a sheath of Glen's letters to Kelli around with me. Free Minds is about not forgetting. And about the conscious decision to abandon nobody.

I write about Michael, not 'cause he is my friend. Not because I've written him letters since he went back to prison. But, because, your people is what you got. And Free Minds, these poems, this work, is a testament to what it means to claim your people when they're going through the worst that might happen.

Gwendolyn Brooks once wrote of a boy named Marc Crawford that his "broken window is a cry for art." What you find in these pages is art crying out for art. Produced under some of the most difficult circumstances, in prisons whose existence are a plague on this nation, this collection is put together from the work of scores of young people who want to be heard. And at bottom of this quest to be heard? Words that sing, that stumble, that hiccup and then soar again. Reading this collection will give you a sense of process, a sense of moving forward. It will remind you of what the power of words can do, and will remind you, ultimately, of why a program like Free Minds Book Club & Writing Workshop is so crucial to the development of young men both before jail cells start calling, and once the tragedies that fill those cells occur.

— Reginald Dwayne Betts
Award-winning author of
Felon, Bastards of the Reagan Era,
A Question of Freedom, and *Shahid Reads His Own Palm*

When we first published this book nearly ten years ago, with the original title *They Call Me 299-359*, we were unprepared for the enormous impact it would have. The book became a vital and potent tool in Free Minds' violence prevention initiative, "On the Same Page." The poems inside were written by incarcerated youth, and openly describe their experiences growing up in poverty, attending under-resourced schools in violence-plagued neighborhoods where drug dealers often served as the most prominent role models, and enduring the isolation of incarceration. At the same time, these poems sing of joy, resilience, first love, connection to family, and dreams for the future. The book affects both readers and writers. Sharing the book with audiences across the city and the nation has helped educate people on systemic racism and root causes of violence and incarceration.

Receiving positive feedback from readers has offered hope and healing and generated an enormous sense of self-worth and emotional connection in the incarcerated writers. It motivates them to write more.

> *I didn't know people out there cared. When you come in here and you've been on the news, you figure people must be scared of you and no longer care about you. When I read what the people (thought about) my poetry, I saw that they didn't think I was an animal, but just a human being who made a bad choice. It made me want to keep on writing!"* ~ *D'Angelo*

As we prepared to publish this new edition of the text, our members decided to change the title to *They **Called** Me 299-359*. This small but significant shift to the past tense demonstrates that the carceral system does not define our poets in the present—and expresses our fervent hope that one day these ID numbers will be relegated to the past as a reminder of what we must never again do to children.

They Called Me 299-359 demonstrates the power of creative self-expression and poetry to build bridges between people incarcerated on the inside, and their community on the outside. This connection and understanding is absolutely imperative if we are to create a better, more equitable and peaceful society for all.

Much has changed in the last 10 years. Then, the term "mass incarceration" had only just been popularized by Michelle Alexander's ground-breaking book, *The New Jim Crow*. Now it is a part of our collective vernacular to describe the explosion in the United States' prison population over the last half century and its disproportionate impact on Black people and communities. Growing awareness and education has led to important progress in justice reform.

The rate of incarceration in this country has decreased over the past decade (although the United States still leads the world). Fewer states now allow children under the age of 18 to be prosecuted in adult court. The Supreme Court eliminated mandatory life sentences without parole for those who committed their crimes as juveniles. And here in Washington, DC, a growing acknowledgement of neuroscience evidence on brain development and criminal responsibility has led to sentencing reform legislation allowing individuals who committed serious crimes as teens, but have served at least 15 years, to seek review. Similarly, in 2018, the DC City Council took the long overdue step of moving youth ages 16 and 17 out of the DC Jail, to a more age-appropriate juvenile detention facility.

Free Minds has greatly expanded our programming since 2011. We have served an additional 1,050 incarcerated or formerly incarcerated people for a total of 1,500 since Free Minds began in 2002. In addition to serving incarcerated youth, we now have book club programs at the DC Jail for: adults pursuing their GED or college education; Spanish-speaking individuals; participants in the Young Men Emerging program, ages 18-25; and women. Through our Reentry Book Club, hundreds of Free Minds members have graduated from job readiness apprenticeships, continued their education or pursued new career goals, and trained as Poet Ambassadors, leading our violence prevention initiative in the DC area and beyond. Free Minds members have become activists working together for themselves and the young people who are coming up behind them. They are hopeful and excited to be part of creating a more just future.

Yet there is still so much work to be done. This year, the tragic killing of yet another Black man, George Floyd, at the hands of police officers, and the nationwide protests that followed have forced Americans to face head-on the brutal history and ongoing reality of racial violence and inequity in our country. During this unprecedented moment of racial reckoning, the voices of those most impacted are the ones that must be most amplified. The poems in this collection are as vital and relevant today as they were in 2011.

We hope that you will read this book and share it widely. Lifting up the voices of those behind the prison walls is an act of hope and solidarity.

— Tara Libert & Kelli Taylor
Co-founders, Free Minds Book Club & Writing Workshop
October 2020

All three of the young men who were chosen to edit this book ten years ago—
Kenneth, Jonas, and Paulo—were serving sentences in federal prison. Together,
they decided what chapter headings would best elicit the stories, emotions and
tone they wanted. A "Call for Submissions" then went out to the more than
200 young Free Minds members from Washington, DC, who were currently
incarcerated in facilities around the country. As the Editorial Board, Kenneth,
Jonas, and Paulo spent the next several months individually poring over poetry
and essays and choosing the writing that resonated the most. The book you
now hold in your hands is their story, told by them. What follows is an interview
conducted in 2011.

What did you think when you were first approached about this project?

Kenneth: I thought, "They must have the wrong guy!" But as the idea
settled on my heart, I thought about the impact this project could have on the
incarcerated young men and especially the outside community. I wanted to be
a part of it because all my life, what people know about me has been negative.
I've changed, but I want my reputation to change as well. This project was
offering me the use of my positive energy to depict something different –
something human and capable of doing productive things.

Paulo: I wanted to do this because I wanted to be heard and not only judged.
I needed a way to express what I have stored since my incarceration seven
years ago.

Jonas: I just knew I couldn't allow this opportunity to be a part of something so
significant pass me by.

What reaction did you have to the hundreds of poems you went through
as an editor?

Kenneth: As I read the poems, I couldn't help but be amazed at all of the talent
that has been caged in, suffocated, because of past mistakes made by juveniles
who were compelled to be someone different than who they actually were…I
read a couple of poems to my celly (cellmate) and he was in awe. It was like the
more I read, the more he wanted to hear. The poems touched me deeply. I was
proud to know these young men were like me, struggling against the demon

of the caged, fighting every day to become something different—something better—something no less than magnificent.

Jonas: It was kind of emotional because I related so much to everything that I read, not only because we're all incarcerated, but because we all have shared such similar life struggles. It's so unclear what it truly means to be a man these days. We're constantly bombarded with false images of what that is. All of us are truly confused and simply trying to find our own way. I could definitely identify with the thirst for knowledge and the desire that all of us have to be righteous.

Paulo: I was amazed to see that people were so willing to share their thoughts and feelings. I wondered if others felt or experienced the things that I struggle with. And it was all right there in their writing!

What role has writing played in your life since you got locked up?

Kenneth: It has made me discover a passion, and allowed me to travel down great avenues and meet so many people I can learn from and grow. Writing has been my late night medicine for loneliness—that force that prevents a physical altercation. Since I have been locked up, writing has been a key to the cage.

Jonas: Writing has been a process of growth for me. Sometimes I go back and read something that I wrote back when I was on the juvenile block and I'm amazed by how far I've come on my path. That in itself is special because sometimes I don't give myself enough credit for the things I've accomplished over the years. Writing has been therapeutic, really vital for me.

Paulo: Writing has reshaped my life and thoughts. It has given my ideas of how to see and live life a positive spin. Through my writing, I have come to speak to the world.

Why do you think it's important for the young men of Free Minds to have a voice?

Jonas: It is *so* important because most of us have been taught, indirectly and some directly, that we don't matter at all. We've been left to fend for ourselves in many ways. Then when we make an error, we are thrown away like trash. I believe that just having a voice is a crucial step in the right direction toward healing the emotional and mental wounds. Everyone wants to feel like they matter.

Paulo: It's imperative that we have a voice. A big part of the problem is that we haven't been bonding with our own community.

What do you hope the reader will take away from the book?

Kenneth: I hope that readers will see that we are more than criminals. We are human beings who have made mistakes.

Do you have any other message for the readers?

Paulo: Yes, I want to ask the readers to pass the book forward.

Where are they now?

Kenneth, now 32, remains incarcerated. He is seeking resentencing under DC's Incarceration Reduction Amendment Act, a bill offering youth charged as adults the opportunity to petition for sentence review after 15 years behind bars.

Paulo, now 35, was deported in 2020 after completing his sentence. He now lives in Bolivia, where he recently started his own business.

Jonas, now 33, was released under the Incarceration Reduction Amendment Act in September 2020 after 17 years. He recently published his own collection of poetry.

THEY CALLED ME 299-359

I COME FROM

My World
By Jonas

I was born into a world
Where the only language men understand is violence
And you have to be trained to go at the drop of a hat
Gun, knife, a bat, or hand-to-hand combat
You never know
You just have to be ready to work with no hesitation

A world where your reputation is everything
It can make or break you
A world where it's best to simply stay in your lane
Play your role
Because when you try to step outside of yourself
It's only a matter of time before people figure out that you don't belong there

And in the world I was born into
Exposure can be a matter of life or death…
I was born into a world where there's no such as thing as meek
Either you're strong or you're weak
Predator or prey
Any chance of finding a grey area is slim to none

A world where manhood is defined
By how many girls you can have sex with
How much money you have
And whether your gun goes off or not

A world where extortions, armed robberies and drug dealings
Are a part of everyday life from sun up to sun down
A world where homicide is likely to be your cause of death
I was born into a world where most people don't know how to cope
With the pain of their struggle
And try to numb it with drugs and alcohol

A world full of so much potential
But the people have endured centuries of brainwashing
That taught them to hate themselves

The young man doesn't value his own life much at all
So he surely won't think twice about taking yours
The young woman will sell her body to you
For a dime rock, a dippa or an e-pill

A world where we're conditioned from early on
To believe that somehow being educated and well spoken
Is lame and un-cool
A world where the gentleman generally doesn't exist
Because we've been terribly misinformed
As to how we're supposed to treat women
I was born into a world where most never escape
And blessed are the few that do…

I was born into a world
That is not as glamorous as the media would have you believe
It's an everyday struggle to simply survive
I just wish all of my brothers and sisters in the struggle the best

I would love to see my world
Rise above the current state of mind
Back into our original consciousness
I've highlighted the problems
But I choose to be part of the solution
I will start by being the change I would like to see in the world
The more I learn, the more I will grow
The more I will rise and shine
And be a source of light for others

Birthplace

By William aka Prince Rich

I was born on the bathroom floor
Born in the worst place
Mama was cryin'
Then came a knock on the bathroom door
You should've seen the look on Grandma's face!
Brought up in the worst place
Taught to always get mine
Even if it was in the worst way

Where money was more important
Than a person breathin' life's breath
I was born in the valley
Walkin' in the shadows of death
Every person from where I'm from
Is in death's race
But I'm gonna stay back in last place
Cuz I ain't tryna be the first
To reach my dirt place

The Day of My Mother's Death
By CW

Her sister's boyfriend killed both of them
I was just a baby
Emotional
Fearful
Worried
Confused
Terrified
Reflecting, I can see it all so clear
The drama
The violence
The whole atmosphere
Unnurtured, unnourished, unattended, unborn
Forecasted, foretold, fore mentioned, forward
Long gone
I revisit the exhibit of her torn and broken spirit
And imagine what would have happened
If, of her own ship she'd been captain
I reminisce on what once was bliss
Filled with gifts, sealed with a kiss
Then I dwell on what was her hell
As her belly swelled to the toll of bells
And it seems like only yesterday
When the child in her went out to play
Now I return to the bed that she had made
And in which she was forced to lay
And I find that if I pray
Trouble don't last always

My Life Story

By Nick

I been locked up since I was 15 years old and I was charged as an adult for carjacking and armed robbery. I already did three years of my time and I have seven more to go. I got caught for what I been doing and been given a lot of time to think about what I did wrong. All my life it feels like I been doing time away from my family. The government always seems to have me in custody.

I want to be a psychologist because I like helping fix people's problems. I figure since I been through a lot, I have a lot in common with people I run into.

When I was five years old, I was the only child of my 25-year-old mother. We always had a good mother-son relationship. In my opinion, she's the coolest mother ever, and I love her to death. My mother wasn't a successful type of woman growing up. She was smoking reefer when she was 17 years old. She couldn't afford to take care of me, so she tried to give me to a group home, but the people there figured she seemed to be doing good herself. I admit, my mother is a beautiful woman and always found a way to have nice clothes.

I'm sure neither of us knew who my father was, but I did have someone who I looked up to as my father. I was even named after him. I always respected him because he took care of a kid that wasn't even his. I lived with him until I was nine years old and moved back in with my mother. Then my mother started to do crack cocaine and hustle drugs too. I was taken away from her and put into a foster home.

I felt so bad, I cried all day. I couldn't believe that I was really gone away from my family. My mother was pregnant with my lil' brother. She started to fall apart. She started to sell her body on the street. It really felt terrible because my friends would see her out there trying to support her habit. My foster mother and her son were physically abusing me. She would keep me from going to school so my teacher wouldn't see my bruises. When I got punished, she made me go in my room all day and night without turning on the light. She took all my books so I wouldn't read. I hated that woman.

My brother was born when I was ten years old. I was adopted then by a woman who I called my godmother. I felt good but I wasn't happy for long. I became sad again because my mother wasn't around. She was killing herself with drugs. I always walked around with my head down. I never smiled. The street I lived on with my godmother was filled with hustlers, prostitutes and everything else you can name. My godmother didn't want me around my mother but I would

4

sneak outside anyway and go look for her. When I found her, we would go sit down on some steps and talk. She would start to make promises that she wouldn't keep. All I wanted was to be with my mother. I wanted her to get herself together so I could be happy again.

I remember my graduation day. I was graduating from the eighth grade and I asked my mother if she would come to my graduation. She said yes. That day, when I walked across the stage I didn't see her. I tried to think up a lot of reasons why she didn't come. I didn't want to believe she really gave up on me or that she just didn't care. A week later my mother was locked up for drugs and sentenced to seven years in prison. That's when my mindset changed. I started to go outside to do criminal activity in my hood. It led me to the spot I'm at now.

I Come From...
By Anonymous

I come from a place that is so beautiful
But even more deadly
Sixteen years of just being present in my domain
I have learned how to survive
I have learned things school can't provide
Even though people say that the 'hood
Is no place to learn and grow and become a man
I see things from a view that few understand
When I'm chillin' wit' my men
Smoking, drinking and just doing me
I know this is where I'm supposed to be
Here on the block, I got a purpose
But to America, I'm just another black person
I know who I am
Because of where I'm from
And if I leave the 'hood
Then who and what will I be?

De Donde Vengo
Por Luís

De donde vengo
El sonido de las balas se escucha
Mas que el canto de los pájaros
Allí la sangre corre por las banquetas

De donde vengo
La violencia es el apellido de las calles
El veneno que existe en la gente
Puede causar que te contagies

De donde vengo
El aroma que se respira es de muerte
Sin importar si es de día o de noche

De donde vengo
No importa la edad pero
Tienes que recordar que el menor error
La vida te puede costar

Where I Come From
By Luís

Where I come from
You hear the sound of bullets
More than the song of birds
There, blood runs over the sidewalks

Where I come from
Violence is the last name of the streets
The virus living in the community
Is something you can catch as well

Where I come from
Death is the smell you breathe in
It doesn't matter if it's day or night

Where I come from
Your age doesn't matter
You have to remember the tiniest mistake
Could cost you your life

YOUNG'UNS

Unknown Victim
By Nick

I was once a boy who was just a paycheck
Being shipped around like the property I was
I was once a boy who cried between the bars
That kept him away from the life he called home
I was once a boy who was lost without his mother
Who was addicted to the pain that was keeping her away
I was once a boy who didn't know the man
That made him from a seed
To have a life by a woman he didn't love
I was once a boy who couldn't explain what life was
Except the hell he was beginning to live
I was once a boy who thought having a gun
Was something to value
I was once a boy who had talent
But sold his dream to society
And got nothing in return but a flight to prison
I was once a boy whose goal was set
To be the man I am today

Hard Times
By DeVonte

Growing up mother on drugs, father in jail
Grandma got high blood pressure
All da weight's on me
A ruler can't even measure my pain
Be calm and stay patient
Everything will get better
Dat's what they told me
But nothing changed yet
I been waiting since they told me
Turned to the streets to find love and joy
The pain turned into anger
And I became "Rude Boy"...
"Rude Boy Selfish"
Became my full name

I Never Thought I'd Be A Hero

By John

Just a normal day in April 2003. I was like 10 years old. Me and my sisters came home from school. My mother was going to get us something to eat from the store. So I turned on the TV and said "Okay, Mom. I got the children."

We were just chillin'. My lil' brother was about two, so I put him to sleep on my bed in the back room. We were watchin' Cartoon Network: me, my sisters Shade, Shakeila, Shakiya and Nijae. Shade's two years younger than me. Shakeila is one year younger than Shade. Shakiya's one year younger than Shakeila, Nijae's one year younger than Shakiya.

My mom called and asked us what we wanted from the store. I said, "We want some pizza," not asking my sisters at all. So my mom said she would be there in an hour. I said, "Okay, Mom. Everything's going to be okay." She said, "Love ya!" I said, "Love you more."

I was getting tired, so I stretched out on the couch and yawned a little. My eyes got heavy and I fell asleep. The phone rang and I woke out of my little nap to answer it. It was my mom. She said she was in line at the store with the pizza and she would be home in like, forty minutes. I said, "Okay."

My sisters were all asleep. I went to go check on my baby brother because I heard him cry. He was fine. I guess he was having a dream. I went back to the couch and fell asleep with the phone on my chest. I was asleep for about ten minutes when I heard a loud noise in the hallway. I went to look out the peephole and it was very black. I opened the door and a cloud of smoke rushed in like a strong wind during a storm. I didn't panic, but it started coming in —a lot of it—and the smoke detector went off, waking up my sisters. They started crying. I rushed them to my mom's room, closed the door and put a towel under it. Then I looked out the window and saw men in big yellow suits on the ground. I opened the window and yelled, "Help! Help!" Next thing you know, a big long ladder came up with a man in a yellow suit with a big black breathing tank on his back. I picked up each of my sisters and gave them to the man. I was about to go myself, but then I thought of my little brother in my room asleep. I rushed to open the bedroom door and the smoke hit me like a punch. My brother was crying like I never heard him before, gasping for air. I picked him up and then ran to the man in the yellow suit. I gave him my little brother.

That's all I remember. I woke up at Children's Hospital Center with a lady in my face sayin', "You are a hero."

I asked the doctor, "Where is my mom?"

"Your mom is not here. She wasn't in the house and y'all are under age to be at home by yourselves."

I said, "So what's that mean?"

He said, "Y'all are going with Child Protective Services."

I said, "What's that?"

Then this lady walked in and said, "Are they ready?"

I said, "Ready for what?"

"Y'all going home." I was so happy, but then she said she wasn't talking about my house. She took us to someone else's house where they washed us up and we put on clothes like PJ's mixed with regular clothes. I cried after I seen all my sisters crying.

In the morning we got split up—two and two and two—to go to different households.

A month later, a lady came and said, "Your mom's waitin' for you outside."

I ran and said "I missed you, Ma!" My mom kissed me and said she was sorry and she would never leave me and my sisters again. I sat in the front seat. She was so proud of me.

This was the happiest day of my life. We went home and washed up and changed into some real clothes. Then she took us to an all-you-can-eat buffet. My whole family was there waitin' for us. Everybody said, "He's a hero!" We had a good time. I'm glad I saved my family from the fire. Thank you, God.

I Remember

By Derrick

I remember when life was all about fun
Football, basketball…never about guns
I used to sit in the house and watch cartoons
Now there's so much death on the evening news
In everything I did, I always excelled
Now I'm stuck in this little-ass cell
I wish I could take back the stupid decision I made
Sometimes when I lie down, I wish my life could fade
I have so much talent, but it's wasted on this
I just sit back and say, "Life's a mess"
I sit in my cell sometimes and cry
'Cause the way I live can't be true—it has to be a lie
So much violence
Need to increase the peace
I wish violence was germs, 'cause I'd keep some bleach
My life has been hell
I wish people could see
Slavery is over, but I'm still not free
Doing wrong is easy, but doing right is hard
My mind travels to different places—today it's on Mars
My world is falling, someone yell "Timber!"
This is just some of the stuff that I remember

The Very Long Journey
By Oscar
This is the story of my journey to the United States.

Before my long journey
I once lived in a far away place
A place filled with harmony and joy
And even though I played with mud-sculptured toys
It was sufficient to me as a little boy
Then suddenly, I was abandoned by my mother
But I still had my father
Then I was taken by my grandmother
Told I was going on a long journey
Told I would live in the land of opportunity
Where I would reunite with my mother
Not told it was also the land of corruption
Not told I'd combat exhaustion, dehydration and starvation
Not told this particular journey I'd have to conquer
For if I quit, I'd be left to die by the smuggler
Not told that at the end of my very long journey
I'd end up in jail
Where I'd embark on an even harder
And longer journey

A Sight I Will Always Remember
By Alvin

When I was about 15, I was going to get my hair cut at the barbershop. I took a short cut past an old closed up school where crackheads and dope addicts used to hang. As I walked through, I saw two police officers beating up a crackhead. The crackhead was hollerin' and screamin', but nobody except me could hear him. I was in shock, and I just stared. Then the policemen saw me, and they stopped. But they kept holding Slim just dangling him over a pole that led to some concrete steps. If they would have dropped him, they would have killed him. I was scared. It's a sight I will always remember.

The Perfect Child
By Delonte

My mother was a fiend
My father was a dealer
You put them together
What do you think they would make?
A child with no remorse
Who is searching for love
So where does he go to find it?
The streets
Where every stray can find love
Even the dumpster can sometimes gets a steak
On the streets my mother was never there
Cared more about the white stone
So what does her child do for attention?
He gets the white stone
Hoping for that same love
My father was a dealer
Never around, chasing money
So what does his son do?
Chase the money by any means necessary
To me I was being the perfect child
For the perfect couple
To society I was a menace
Undeserving of forgiveness or understanding
Sometimes I'm full of hate
Other times, I just want my parents to care
Still trying to be
The perfect child

Young Forever

By SN

I want to be young forever
Not who I am right now
But the kid I was in my past
I miss my old life and the good old days
If I had one wish
I'd wish to be a kid again
For forever
Never worry about anything
Just smile, laugh and play
Around everybody who loves you
Right now I feel like
I would do anything to get my old life back
I just want to be young forever

TITLE 16

(Title 16 of the DC Code allows for juveniles to be charged and tried as adults for certain offenses.)

Confined as a Youth

By Antwon

When you think about childhood
You 'posed to be able to smile
But never in my life was I taught how
I was always around anger that led to pain
I was always confined
At least that's how it felt to my brain
The streets not only took me, but they took my mother too
Confined as a youth, so tell me what I 'posed to do?
Some people say they love the streets because the game is all they know
I will never label myself until I give myself time to grow
And sometimes I wonder why do it always have to be me?
Then I hear my great grandma's voice saying
"You wasn't the only one that wasn't free"
It's crazy how people put lies in our heads
Trying to get us to believe this is who we are
When, for real, every living thing was made to be a star
I hope one day we will see there's no limit to what we can do
But until that day comes, I'm here on earth, "confined as a youth"

When I Got Arrested

By Marc

I was walking to the trashcan to throw my chips away
When I was stopped and handcuffed in front of my neighborhood store
I had an adult warrant
And everybody seen me getting arrested
The handcuffs were as tight as a screw on a bike
My stomach felt like the Drop Zone at King's Dominion
My head pounded like a left hook from Ali
Now I'm here in jail
I feel dumb as a doorknob

When I Get Sentenced
By Alexis

When I get sentenced
Where will you be?
Will you be on the first row?
On the first bench, praying for me?
If I lose and when all's said and done
Will you still be in my corner
As if I had won?
Or will you start your new life
With the next one?
I know none of this is your fault
But if I were taking a vacation
Instead of going to court
You would be with me at that airport
Right or wrong?
The way I love you
Will never change
But do you love me the same?

Urgent Notice
By JohnQuan

It's kinda' sad how they label us
Black juveniles, I mean
Want us to do right
But provide us with nothing!
I'm 17 — that's young
Not close to old age
Yet they tell me my life's over
After reading the first page
Jail is the last stage
So they don't care what we do
Want to know how I know or how I can tell?
Because I fit a description so I'm thrown in jail
I been here one month
What happens next, I can't tell
This is just a short memo
Of juvenile life
Housed in the adult jail

A Youth's Outlook
By Robert aka Rah-Rah

I broke the law and accept what I've done
In return I get 9 years for a lighter that looked like a gun
Listen to the outlook from one of the blessed youth
I said the blessed youth
From the blessed youth that's been fed nothing but lies
Nowhere close to the truth
The things we took up are guns, knives and bats
Yeah, we be armed and strong
But how do you know it's not right if you're being taught wrong
Who cares enough to listen and slow down?
To understand the youth's struggle?
Who really, honestly wants to help?
Is it you?
I asked, is it you?
A youth's outlook is what I'm trying to share
A youth's outlook is priceless and rare
A youth's outlook should be carefully examined
A youth's outlook is like fire from a cannon
A youth's outlook from a young inquiring mind
A youth's outlook while locked up and doing time
One thing I ask of you before I end this
Listen
I just ask that you hear me out
Try to understand

My Life In Ages and Stages
By TB

6 –Father dies
7 – Start being disrespectful
8 – Start playing sports
9 – Run away from home
10 – Don't listen
11 – Get outta control
12 – Get put out of school
13 – Motha' is thru with me
14 – Start to drink and smoke weed
15 – Get locked up
16 – Get Title 16 and come over to the jail

LOCKDOWN

Slowly Fading Away
By Jonas

I feel like I'm slowly fading
Like smoke into thin air
In constant search of a caring soul
But no one really cares
It's rare to find a genuine heart, truly sincere and kind
Especially when you end up in a predicament like mine
Snatched away from society at a very young age
With no guidance and no structure, I was living in a haze
But the past is done and gone and my future seems bleak
I'm slowly fading away
Like a drunk when he drinks
I think this life is worth living
Sometimes it's hard to tell
It's like I was born into Satan's hands, then cast into hell
My potential is at a peak, where I'm beginning to see
But twenty years from now, who knows where I'll be
Still locked in a cell where my potential and worth
Is a "was"— a thing of the past
My dreams and goals are vast, things I aspire to achieve
It's a daily struggle for me to continue to believe
To believe that I could actually be more than a thug
To believe that a woman still wants to give me a kiss with her love
Still wants to see me smile and tell me I'm so cute
To see that I've blossomed into a wonderful man
Though I didn't have rich roots
Locked away like this, everyone seems to forget
I'm slowly fading away
Into a bottomless pit
Out of sight, out of mind, damn it's a shame
Sometimes I wonder if certain people even remember my name
In a place like this you become very aware
Before, ignorance was bliss and you don't know to be scared
I feel like I have so much to offer
But am I really even here?
Time waits for no one, and no one sees my tears
I'm ripe and ready for whatever

Chapter 4

I'm 21 years young
Sometimes my soul feels 80, like it's almost done
I'm slowly fading away
Into a mist of confusion
Constantly wondering if my life is just an illusion

Mind Full of Holes
By Derrick

I'm sitting in the hole doing time
Not the hole in jail, but the hole in my mind
Trying to get a grip on the edge of the cliff
But my fingertips always seem to slip
With my eyes wide open, all I see is darkness
Wonder how could I be so heartless
Because there isn't a human alive
That would cause himself this much pain
Everything I'm going through, I fault myself
Maybe I'm a lost soul that lost hope
On a lost road
Or maybe I'm the devil in the flesh
That would explain why my life's a mess
It's like I'm slippin' further into insanity
And everyone and everything I hate passionately
Sometimes I try to change my ways
But it seems like the good side of me is caged
And I leave my anger that's on fire ablaze
Not even the fire department could put it out
Sometimes this all takes a toll
Welcome to my mind
That's full of holes

Dear Excitement
By Arthur

Dear Excitement:

Wazup! I was just thinking about you. I would love if you were here with me, because I need you, especially right now. I be feeling like I can never be like you. I am always hanging with your enemy, Upset. I am tired of being around him. He makes me sick to my stomach. That's another reason I need you. You will make my day. I miss you.

Write back ☺

Sincerely yours,
Arthur

Jail
By DeAnte

Thirty minutes in the shower, and thirty minutes to use the phone
Then back in a cell for 23 hours, I can't wait 'til I go home
The food is disgusting, the air is stale
They record my phone calls, and read through my mail
Every time I come in this place, I feel worthless and cursed
Some guys may like it in here, but I think it's the worst
People are disrespectful and the inmates carry knives
The water is recycled and makes my skin break out in hives
The slippers hurt your feet, and the mattresses are thin
The deodorant doesn't work and the toothpaste makes you stink
Some guys are very talented artists and poets
But being trapped behind these walls, they never get to show it
In here it's like you're dead, forgotten, a myth
It's like you never were important, you never did exist
A 6x9' wall to wall, better known as a cell
This is how it is every time I come to jail

Broken Way

By Joshua

I am walking on a broken way
Alone with no one by my side
I search for a friend
But I find none to walk with me
Life's troubles come as a thundering storm
I am caught in the middle of it
With nothing to protect me
From its dangerous winds
I am caught up in the air
Not knowing where I'll be blown
But when I land back on the ground
I'm back where I started
Back on the broken way alone

Incarcerated

By Robert aka Rah-Rah

Brick walls, fences, and razor wire criss-crossed in a bind
Intense feelings 'cause remorse is the punishment of crime
No warmth lives here but the wind that chills
So much counterfeit 'cause the fake outweighs the real
It's not just those behind walls and locked doors that are doing time
But in the outside world, people are incarcerated in the mind
Not always what it seems, sometimes it's a blessing
Only what you make of it, not always unpleasant
But will you gain strength? Or will you bend?

Crossing Lines

By PCD

This poem describes when a fight breaks out in prison and the alarm goes off. In a penitentiary, small things can become big.

The sun burns the day
Isolated souls roam about
Eyes of the sky stare down
All movements cease

Hearts begin to pound
Thoughts begin to run wild
Four souls struggle for force
Everyone looks around

They scatter or rush in
Hungry and thirsty they act
Few sympathize
Some demonize

Bam...Bam...
Bodies hit ground
Few look around
Some squat
Many lie facedown

Momentum kicks in
The sun continues to feed the day
Isolated souls rise and roam again
A war has been ignited for the day

Reunite

By William aka Prince Rich

Alone I wait
As my heart starts to race
Longing for the day
That I am reunited
With the ones I love
Dance, play and marvel at the stars above
Me and my sons
Lion and cubs
But for now I'm alone
That's my plight
I'm in the hole in the dark
Lookin' for the light
Waitin' for the day that I can get it right
And finally reunite

Lockdown

By Talib

Being on lockdown is stress
No movement, no visits
And no school to progress
You must free your mind
Because your body's locked in a box
And if you let it get the best of you
You'll find yourself in the dark
Exercise, read and write
That's what I do almost every night
This is the incarceration life
So you must man up
Unlock your mind
And don't waste your time

BEHIND THE NUMBER (OR WHO I REALLY AM)

Fish Outta' Water
By DC

I feel like I'm drowning on land
I'm in a place I can't understand
I need to get back to my water
Where are the sharks when you need 'em?
Here the creatures get mad when you don't feed 'em

I'm suffocating from this air
I floated out of my sea because I lived without a care
Mama fish told me, Sista' fish told me
In jail I'ma ugly fish, even though I'ma goldie!

I have learned to walk, even though
Swimming was the right thing to do
I'm slowly dying, my face is turning blue
Dear Great Sea I'm coming back to you
Soon, very soon I hope to make it
Because a fish on land – CAN'T TAKE IT

Gasping for air, and I'm not acting
Because outta' the water
I'm missing in action!

Wrong Sight of a Young Black Man
By Juan

If you could really see me
You would not be afraid of me
If you would just open your eyes and see
You would not misjudge me
Yeah, I'm young, black, brave and bold
But that still don't give you the right
To misjudge my soul
I think that when you see me, you are scared
Scared that I'll be something great or powerful

I can smell your fear
But don't be afraid of me
Encourage me
Encourage me to be a better person
If you will really see me
You will see the hunger
I want to be better for me and my family
All that you see is what this environment gave me
But one day you'll see the best man
That I am striving hard to be

They Call Me 299-359
By DW

Orange jumpsuit, shower shoes and an armband
Guilty by appearance and judged by my race
Guilty until innocent in the words of a D.A.
Lost in a cold dream called prison
Four sharp corners, eggshell paint, dusty gray floor
No lights and a filthy toilet
No tears, just my pen in action
They call me 299-359
Correctional officers view me as a stupid savage
I push the pen so that I remain happy
Mama and Daddy, these are the unspoken words of your baby's diary
My orange jumpsuit and number are only the book cover
So please don't judge
My words are as pure as gold
Not aware of the success these lines hold
I operate this pen to fight the war mentality
So please understand me
They call me 299-359
Orange jumpsuit, shower shoes and an armband

Antes Escuchaba

Por Luís

Antes escuchaba a algunos decir que quisieran ser como yo
Aunque sea por un día
Si alguien se pusiera en mis zapatos
Y diera un par de pasos por donde yo he caminado
Yo se que una hora después
Se estuvieran dando por vencido

Antes escuchaba a gente decir que tengo ojos bonitos
Pero si miraran como yo miro vieran que no todos los colores brillan
Lograran comprender que mis ojos pequeños
Son para el dolor esconder

Antes escuchaba que era afortunado
Y que nada me faltaba y que todos deseaban estar en mis zapatos
Me gustaria que ellos pudieran ver que
Solo estoy sobreviviendo todo lo que en la vida me a tocado vivir
Soy el de los zapatos grandes
El de los sueños destruidos
Y que aunque el año no sido bueno
Siempre esta viviendo

I Used to Hear

By Luís

I used to hear people say that they wanted to be like me
Even if only for a day
If someone were to put themselves in my shoes
And walk a few steps where I have been
I know that an hour later
They would be giving up
I used to hear people say that I have beautiful eyes
But if they looked where I look they would see that not all colors shine
They would come to understand that my small eyes
Are a place for pain to hide
I used to hear that I was lucky

That I had it all and everyone wanted to be in my shoes
I wish they could see that
I am only surviving everything life has handed me to live
I am the one with the big shoes
And the shattered dreams
And although this hasn't been a good year
I am one still living

I DREAM

College
By PJ

Most young poets talk about the ghetto
But I'll talk about college
That's where I wanna be to obtain some knowledge
I wanna be out from behind bars
In a college class getting ready for the future
And learning from the past
People think prison makes you change your ways
But in reality it only makes you worse
'Cause there are inmates all around you with a criminal thirst
We wanna steal, rob and kill
Because we think there's nothing to look forward to
In college I can study black history
But behind bars my people are a mystery
I am locked up for a robbery
My father died in one
I don't know what made
My dumb ass pick up a gun
Now when I get released
I wanna go to college
Because there's no point in living
If we don't have knowledge!

Never
By Joshua

Never had a girl before
Wish I did have a girlfriend
I really want one bad
I need a companion
Someone to talk to at night
Someone I can love
One that understands me
Wish I could get a girl now
But of course, I can't
So I'm prayin' to God
To one day
Bring someone into my life
To love me for me

The Best Dream
By Andrew

The C.O.* came to my cell and said, "Pack your bags!" I was in shock. I was asking myself, how was I going to get home? The C.O. took me down to the front gate. I looked and I saw my mother and the rest of my family. I was dressed in an orange jumper. I ran through the gates and gave my mother a big fat hug and kissed her. I mean, I sat right there and hugged my mother for about five or six minutes! In the car my family started asking about how it was behind the wall, but I didn't want to talk about it.

I was hungry, but it was like they already knew. My mother said, "We are going to the all-you-can-eat buffet in Virginia." I was glad and blessed because I hadn't eaten food from the streets in a long time. When we arrived at the buffet, man, I ate good! I ate like I hadn't eaten in about two or three months. After coming back from the buffet we went to our new home. It was out in Maryland. Man! The house was big and pretty. We went in and it was laid out. I had my own room. Everything I needed was already there. I lay on my big soft bed and started to go to sleep. I hadn't slept in a bed in a long time. I closed my eyes and...boom! The dream was over.

My cell door opened. It was time for breakfast. I thought to myself, what a great dream I just had. I promised myself that day is going to come, and I am going to do everything I can never to come back to a place like this.

* Correctional Officer

Wasted
By Curtis

They say time waits for no one
So I don't think about the time
But I think back about a lot of things
I think about all that I will do
When I go home
It's 2:38 AM and I'm all alone
I remember people saying
If you have a dream, chase it
But something inside of me is saying
Face it...your time has just been wasted

The Calling
By Christopher

As I sat in my room I heard a strange noise
Someone calling me — I asked, who's there?
And a voice replied
It's me, your mind
We need to have a talk
Why don't you use me when you should?
To escape your imprisonment in that place you call 'hood'
To go to college and computer school
To become that person you dream about at night
The one with a nice job and a car and a wife
Two pretty kids and a big old house
With a two car garage for you and your spouse
These are all the things you can have
If you just use me and stay on the right path

Falling Star
By Kenneth

I wish on a falling star
While I watch it fall from my window
Memories instantly play back
As I wish for the days when life was simple
Childhood games when worry was missing
And my ignorance was bliss
Not quite eligible for the lesson life taught
But I might be wishing too far back
Or probably can't remember when life was at ease
Or maybe these memories don't exist
But still I wish to be relieved
I wish to escape the madness
The stressful days and restless nights
The loneliness I feel
When I need to be told that everything is all right
But the star is still falling
My chance to wish isn't over
So I wish one wish
For all of this to be just an illusion

Dreams Mixed with Felonies
By Michael

I have dreams mixed with felonies
For the rest of my life
I will be judged, stereotyped, and looked at differently
But I have a dream
And I believe in it
I dream to reach that bright light
That shines at the end of a darkened tunnel
It may take me some time, but I'll make it there
Should I be looked at so differently
Because my dreams come with a few felonies?
Should I be judged for the rest of my life?
I'm only human, just like everyone else
And we make mistakes
The important thing is what do we do next
We must learn from it
As Obama ran to become the first African American president
I often heard the word "change"
I know I can't change the world
But I can change my old ways
My dreams will start to become a reality
At that very moment when you open your eyes
And decide not to judge me
For the wrong that I may have done in the past
But commend me for the good that I do now and in the future
On that day you will see me emerge from a darkened tunnel
Into that limelight in front of thousands of people
To help try to make a change
By helping lead others away from a life that I once chose
I have dreams mixed with felonies…

Becoming Clean

By Tune

Every night I dream
Dream of leaving the past and becoming clean
I despise the days of misfortune
Which turned my dreams into conflict
Every night I dream
I dream of a different upbringing
But harsh reality sets in
And with my life I continue to bet
To lose instead of win…
Every night I dream
Of becoming
A legal citizen
A loyal friend
A good son
To the father that never did wrong
Every night I dream
That I stopped sinning
That I became a brother
That rejoices in being a father
But my steps still seem to be errors
My steps that are on thin feathers
Feathers snap and now my steps are disasters
Every night I dream
Hoping one day I will feel free

LOVE STORIES

Amor y Pasión

Por Luís

Soy enamorado del amor
Por eso es que en mis poemas amor es
el tema principal
Escribir del amor es mi pasión
Creo en el amor y en que estoy
enamorado
Escribiendo es como demuestro mi
amor
Y aunque el amor es como una palabra
que para el mundo no existe
Porque la gente frecuente solo sufre
desilusiones,
Incluso hay gente que prefiere que no
menciones lo que es amor
Soy un amante del amor y trato de
averiguar lo que en verdad es amar
Estudio las diferentes formas de amor
Y sé que no en todos se puede confiar
Todavía, nunca pretendo no
enamorarme
Vivo enamorado
De los recuerdos que en mi mente están
presentes
No hay edades para dejar o comenzar a
enamorarse
Un gran deseo que tengo es que la gente
No deje de creer en el amor
Y que se olviden del rencor
Yo alimento bastante a mi corazón con
mucho amor
Amor es la palabra que en mi mente
Sustituye dolor y rencor
Y en el nombre del amor
Siempre escribiré

Love and Passion

By Luís

I am in love with love
That's why in my poems, love is the
principal theme
To write about love is my passion
I believe in love and I am in love
Writing is how I show my love
And although love is a word that
doesn't exist in the world
Because people often suffer only
disappointments
There are even those who prefer that
you don't mention what love is
I am a lover of love and I try to find
out what it really means to love
I study the different forms of love
And I know that you can't trust all of
them
Still, I never pretend not to fall in love
I live in love
With those memories that are present
in my mind
There aren't ages to stop or start
falling in love
I have a great desire that people
Do not stop believing in love
And that they forget resentment
I feed my heart with love
Love is the word that in my mind
Replaces pain and anger
And in the name of love
I will always write

My Butterfly
By Antonio

Understand, me and you are like butterfly wings
Separated, but always seem to end up back together
You mean so much to me
When the night comes
When the moon rises
And the sun falls
Then we fly
For the love of butterflies

The Day I Met My Girl
By D'Angelo

I got on the D8 Bus because I was too lazy to walk up the hill. It smelled like a mixture of perfume, cigarettes, and old people. As I got to the back of the bus, the moon was shining on her. The bus was crowded and her school books were on the chair so I just stood there. She looked at me out of the corner of her eye and said, "What, you allergic to girls? You can sit by me." She moved her books. As we came to my stop and finished our conversation, we exchanged numbers. We fell in love but never told each other until I got locked up.

Talking to Love
By Davon

Love, I think I know you, but really I don't
I want to tell a girl about you
But I can't, so I won't
Love, I used your name so many times in vain
Told girls I loved them
But the whole time it was a game
Love, let's take a long walk or sit down and talk
Let me know how I can tell the real you and the fake apart
Love, there's this girl that I'm with that I don't ever want to depart
Love, let me know how you make people feel and act
So next time I use your name it can be from the heart

Wishin'

By Nadar

Wishin' it was still us
Wishin' I never cheated
To make us break up
Wishin' I was better
Wantin' to be the best
Wishin' there was a stronger word than "sorry"
So I could be that
Wishin' we could go back
To the very start
Just wishin'

Blinded

By Curtis

The good and bad times
We've made it through them all
I can't see what's going on
Physically, I have 20/20 vision
I'm talking emotionally
With my heart's eyes closed
I'm scared I might fall
I'm blinded

I Carry Your Heart

By TE

I carry your heart with me
Because without your heart
There's no me
That's why I carry it
So I can breathe
Here is the deepest secret
Nobody knows
Without you
There is no me

In Jail Or In Someone Else's Arms

By Antwon
Dedicated to my ex-girl Ce-Ce: You was right, I was wrong

When you thought about me in the mid hours of the night,
where was I?
> In jail or in someone else's arms

When you wanted me, needed me and yearned for me,
where was I?
> In jail or in someone else's arms

When you held your stomach, looked into the mirror, and thought about our future,
where was I?
> In jail or in someone else's arms

When you told me that when I'm ready, my bed will always be made,
where was I?
> In jail or in someone else's arms

When you cried out in pain as our baby's blood rushed out of you,
where was I?
> In jail or in someone else's arms

When you sorrowed and couldn't believe our baby was gone,
where was I?
> In jail or in someone else's arms

When you told me I was a dog and that this was the last straw,
where was I?
> In jail or in someone else's arms

When you gave up on our love and decided not to trust,
where was I?
> In jail or in someone else's arms

Al Enamorarme

Por Luís

Al enamorarme nadie me advirtió que el amor traía consecuencias
Al enamorarme yo cree ilusiones, entregué mis sentimientos por completo

Cuando nos conocimos no me advertiste que pasaría
Si algún día tu olvidarías las ilusiones que tu creaste
Tampoco me advertiste que mi corazón sufriría

Al enamorarme nadie me advirtió que el amor traía consecuencias
Al enamorarme yo cree ilusiones, entregué mis sentimientos por completo

Cuando tu me decías que me querías no me advertiste que el amor mi vida cambiaría
Al besarme no me advertías que una separación cambiaría mi forma de pensar

Al no advertirme me dejaste ir a la guerra sin armas para sobrevivir
No me contaste que necesitará un mapa para saber donde tenía que caminar
Me dejaste solo sin explicar que el amor tiene consecuencias

Falling in Love

By Luís

Falling in love no one warned me that love brought consequences
Falling in love I believed illusions and gave my feelings completely

When we met you didn't warn me what would happen
If one day you would forget the illusions you had believed
Nor did you warn me how my heart would suffer

Falling in love no one warned me that love brought consequences
Falling in love I believed illusions and gave my feelings completely

When you told me you loved me you didn't warn me that love would change my life
When you kissed me you didn't warn me that a separation would change the
   way I thought

By not warning me you left me to go to war without weapons of survival
You didn't tell me I would need a map to know where I had to walk
You left me alone without explaining that love has consequences

DEAR FAMILY

In Memory
By Chris

On June 10, 2007
My life was over
That was the day
My mother died
And that whole day
I was broken-hearted
My family told me
That it was God's work
But at the time
I thought it was my fault
Because I got locked up
But everything will be all right
Because the last thing I told her
Was I love you

Word To Lil' Brova'
By Everett

Well dis is what I got to say
Don't go out there running the street like me everyday
I mean just look at where I am at
And where I could have been
Could have been at home with y'all
But I'm in jail
And guess what?
I failed you as a big brother
I was there physically
I fought for you, woulda killed for you
Got beat up for you
Even got jumped for you
As a big brother
I was there to protect and believe in you
But criminal ways put me in awkward positions
And so I wasn't really there for you

41

But as of today my criminal ways are finally finished
What I'm really trying to say is
Don't be like me
Be better than me
Show me that running the streets don't run in our family
Don't be no fool like me
Not going to school
Breaking every one of Mom's rules
Show me that you can get A's and B's
And get on the honor roll
Give Mom a rest
She don't need no more stress on her chest
She already has enough coming from me
That's why she always has swollen feet
But just tell her prop up her feet
'Cause I'll be home any day now
Word to Lil' Brova'
Don't give your soul to the streets

Stole My Heart
By DeVonte

I showed you all my love
But more and more you did drugs
You raised us well
But when we started going to jail
Your love for us fell
When we were out in public
And men looked at chu'
I was looking back mugging
You were more than someone
Who brought me into this world
You were my provider
My mother, my father
Growing up, since I can remember
You always were on my side
But the drugs made you and me divide
Some nights I wanna cry
What did these drugs do to my mova?
They stole my heart

But no matter what, Ma
I will always love you

My Hero
By DeShawn

You my sister, best friend, straight up
You my, kidney, lung, rib—I'd give up my liver
These nights cold wit' out you, so I'm bound to shiver
Knowin' you and Shawn, y'all sittin' up in Sizzler
Wit' steak smothered in butter
A couple a shakes and some cake
And Antwinette wit' y'all
I know she scrape the plate
Crack a smile, a laugh for me
'Cause I know you 'bout to cry
You got a future on your hands
Man, I see it in your eyes
Honesty in your lies
Beauty in your face
Whenever I hopped out of line
You put me in my place
Most everything I know
I learned it from you
I love your sense of style
The world should be furnished by you
I see no wrong in the things that you do
If somethin' happen to my dawg
My life would be through
Since kids you been Wonder Woman to me
Before you was twelve
You everything I wanted to be
We known as sister & brova wit' style and looks
I was known for my fists, you was known for the books
You a strong, black woman and you ain't even eighteen
Ask Grandma and Daddy
Man, they know what I mean
Two words to describe you—dependable and strong
When you talk, I take heed
Cause you never steer me wrong

You're a natural with kids and never gave birth
You're an angel from above, a gift to this earth
You got no idea how you've affected my life
And you're one of the reasons why I'm gonna do right
But not just for you, I'ma do it for me
'Cause 1901 D Street is not where I wanna be
It took a couple of years
But now I realize
You're more than Big Sis'
You're a hero in my eyes

Ghost Dad
By Juan

Here one day and gone the next
Where did he go? My little voice vexed
Growing up without a dad, that I did
So I grew up a fatherless kid
Every three years he would call me
And every three years he told the same lie
He said he was going to pick me up
But he never did, so I guess he ain't give a care
Only time he called was when he got locked up
I was always happy to talk to him, it felt like good luck
When he finally came to see me
I thought I was dreaming
Wow! I finally saw my dad
My feelings were no longer bad
A spitting image of him, that's what I looked like
When I seen his face, I couldn't believe my sight
As soon as I closed my eyes, he was gone from the light
I could no longer see him, I tried with all my might
Here one minute and gone the next
Where did he go? My little voice vexed
My dad, he left me, he left me alone
So I said forget him
I'll learn to be grown on my own

Baby Boy

By DeVonte

I love you with all my heart
The only way I'll leave you
Is if death splits us apart
I can see you'll be the wise one out of da bunch
Sitting at lunch wit' the girls
Instead of wit' jailbirds smoking blunts
My Junior
My heart
The strings to my guitar
My love for you stretches so far
Binoculars couldn't see where it stops
The best thing to have in this world
Is real love

Healing

By TB

I wrote this poem for my Dad (AKA "Hamma") when he was sick. He passed away while I was locked up. R.I.P., Dad.

This poem is not a poem for fun
This is a poem that will tell how much
I care for someone (my father)
I miss and love him so much
Right now I hate that we're not in touch
I miss tellin' him about my day on the phone
Or being laid back watching a movie at home
My father means so much to me 'cause he taught me a lot
He's the reason I know I will survive in life
Ever since I was small, he always told me to do right
But now that he's getting older, it's my turn to take care of him
Ayyy, Hamma, I'ma keep bangin' with you
'Til all the nails in

Show Me Da Way

By Gerald
Dedicated to Anna Grandma

It hurts not to be home
It kills me to know you are alone
By yourself, worried about me
But you always been like dat, since I was three
You love me like crazy and I know dat you do
Nothing can stop what we have
'Cause it's always been me and you
You said when I get out we are going to have a talk
But when I get out I want you to show me how to walk
Walk the right road, dat's going straight to the heavenly gates
Show me what must be done before it's too late
I know you're going to heaven and dat's easy to say
I can't say dat for myself, but I want to be with you
So please, show me da way

To My Family and Friends

By DeAnte

A deep disappointment, I know I have been
I have failed them once again
My family and friends do right
Righteous is all they ever asked
But I never seen the righteous path
I was always moving too fast
To my mother, don't feel bad
I know you did your best
You have shown nothing but love
And all I caused you was stress
"Praise God and He will guide you"
Is what you always taught
But I chose the wrong way
So my downfall is my fault
I wish I would have just listened
But now I'm paying the price

I was blind to the fact
That people really cared about my well being
The love was always there
But I don't deserve the love
It just doesn't seem fair
That after all the pain I caused them
They are still here
So atrocious, audacious
My actions seem so helpless
Inconsiderate of others
I have always been selfish
But my loved ones never left
It just made them love me more
All I did was hurt them
What do they love me for?
Why do they still care for me as much as they do?
I don't know
But to them I have a lot to prove
I must prove that I can do it
And they didn't waste their time
They have nurtured my life goals
Now it's up to me to shine
I must focus on my dreams
Because there is nothing I can't do
For all the love and support that was shown
I would really like to thank you

DC STREETZ

DC is a City of Life
By Anthony

Man, DC is a city to love
But it's not until you are behind bars
That you understand
The way the air feels
Or the way the concrete holds its place
As you look out your cell window
You understand that the city is alive
The wind as its lungs
The concrete as its skin
And the rain as its tears
Then you truly understand
That DC makes up a person's body

Summertime in DC
By Alvin

When I think about summer this is what comes to mind
Girls with booty shorts showing their legs and shaking their behinds
When I think about summer this is what I see
Bees and blackjacks flying around trying to sting me
When I think about summer this is what I feel
A lot of people I seen in the winter will probably be killed
When I think about summer this is what I know
My mother will be on the grill cooking over a lot of coal
When I think about summer I know the sun will shine
When I think about summer this is what comes to mind

My Fault
By Bernard

Is it my fault I grew up around crud living?
The block can turn you into a man
But now I'm drug dealing
My best friend's mama smokin' buttas
Should I serve her?
Or let my pockets stay broke because I love her
Lil' sisters going crazy
Man they're wildin' out!
Cuz I was in jail when Mama died
God, I'm cryin' out!
Is it my fault, I've got a lust for material things?
Addiction to fast money
Makes me love pitchin' to fiends
Everybody wants change
That's what Obama says
You gotta get it how you live
That's what my Mama would say
My mind gone insane
Man, that's what the doctor says
Now go where I live, then go see where that doctor stays
His house looks a lot different than my project building
You could neva' understand this project living
Floor after floor there's a story in these walls
The only place you can get rich, then go to jail, then lose it all
So is it my fault that I did what I did?
Lil' babies havin' babies raisin' project kids
Is it my fault I want a different type of living?
Yeah, it's my fault
Cuz I'm just gettin' it how I'm living

Uptown
By Darrell

A neighborhood I know very well
Has changed my mind about life
It's a neighborhood

That makes you think that life is all about
Selling drugs, having sex with girls, doing drugs,
skipping school, busting hammers, beefing,
staying out all night and day,
fighting each other,
going to the go-go,
and most importantly…
getting money
I now know what life is really about
And this neighborhood makes me sick
I feel sorry for the little kids in this neighborhood
Because they're going to see all the things I seen

Missin' You

By Jonas

You were my right hand man
At first I couldn't understand
After a while I had to let the tears burst
I felt cursed
Because we used to roll together
We balled together
We always stood tall together
And now you're gone
I understand where we went wrong
We leaned towards the wrong direction
Now I'm singin' this song
If ya' think I can't feel your pain, ya' dead wrong
I'm steady in this game, but sometimes I feel insane
I miss ya' man
Always knew that you were the best
Always wondered why those bullets had to put you to rest
Two to the chest, three to the belly, I was so weak
Standing there watchin' you bleed, I could barely speak
It's been three years, but you know, I don't wonder no more
Things have changed, and God already ordained
I'm resting in peace, 'cause I know we'll meet again
For I know we were both God's children
One love
R.I.P.

The Happiest Day of My Life/Where I Went Wrong
By BF

June 3, 2004 was the morning of my sixth grade graduation. I woke up at 7:45, took a shower, and got dressed. I wore a black, baby blue, and white tuxedo, with some white and black dress shoes—I looked real sharp, like I was going to a wedding or something. My mother cooked me my favorite breakfast: strawberry waffles and sunny side up eggs with orange juice. After eating, I grabbed my tuxedo jacket and headed for the car.

In the car my mother clamored with joy, saying how happy she was. My brothers were getting the camera ready. When we arrived at the elementary school, I was greeted by my principal and teachers and was taken away to my assigned seat. When the program began, my heart skipped a beat because of my stage fright. As I approached the stage, the audience grew very loud with cheering and people chanting my name.

I grabbed my certificate. The crowd calmed down and just like that, the graduation ceremony was over. We went to eat at the country breakfast across the Woodrow Wilson Bridge. That was one of the happiest days of my life.

But soon reality set in. See, my graduation was on a Monday, and the following Saturday night, my best friend Lil' D was killed on his front porch. Earlier that day, Lil' D and I were riding our trick bikes. Mine was a purple, silver, and black Mongoose with silver and black pegs. Lil' D's was a red, black, and gold Mongoose, with gold pegs. We raced to the Eastover shopping center to buy new inner tubes for our bikes. After that we went our separate ways.

Later that night, I heard about 16 to 18 gunshots. They were loud, too, like they were really close. I decided to ride my bike to Lil' D's house. I rarely paid any attention to the gunshots because you heard them every night. As I approached his neighborhood though, it was taped off and police and detectives were everywhere. I saw Lil' D's sister and brother standing there crying. I rode towards them and asked what happened.

His sister replied, "He's gone, he's gone."

I said, "Who's gone?"

She said "D is. Lil' D's gone," and cried harder.

I put my bike down and closed my eyes and prayed to God that it was a dream and that I would wake up. But no, it wasn't a dream. It was life—real life. We were so young. All I could say as I broke down in tears was, "Why D? Why Lil' D? God..."

My mother had already heard the news. She came to pick me up and to give condolences to his family. The funeral was one week later. It didn't look like the Lil' D I knew in the casket. It was over, my life would now turn into a nightmare. That whole summer I did bad stuff. I started smoking, stealing, just doing anything.

The summer passed, and I started the 7th grade. I fought that whole year, smoked more weed, and started to drink. The next year was even worse, I did anything bad a thirteen year-old could do. I carried weapons and started fights. High school is where I really messed up though. I started getting locked up, and now I'm waiting to be sentenced for a serious crime.

I never really sat back and asked myself "Why did I change?" But as I write about this part of my life, I recognize the reason. It was because my best friend was killed. If he was still alive, I wouldn't be here at all.

Every year on his birthday, we all celebrate by smoking and drinking. But now that I'm not high I realize that Lil' D wouldn't want us to do this, not at all. He would have wanted me to finish school and be someone in life. Hopefully I will.

Tears of a Clown
By DC

They say if you don't stand for something
You'll fall for anything.
So they defend a block or region
But don't defend what's inside themselves
I'm gonna call their bluff
Because I know what's up
They smile, laugh, and try to act tough
But the whole time I see the feelings
That they are trying to hide
They're jelly beans!
Hard outside and soft on the inside
Can't fool me, I see right through you
You still portray the smile that clowns do
You're smiling to keep from crying
And while your act is still alive
YOU are steadily dying

Life in D.C.
By SS

I hear gunshots, loud music and police sirens
I smell the smell of weed, black and milds, and jacks
I taste wings and fried rice from Sam's carryout
I see my friends outside, girls leaving school
And the metro bus passing
I feel that this is the place I want to live
I wouldn't feel right living anywhere else

Talk With My Straps
By Kenneth

I remember when you came into my life
I was younger than I am today
Why did I want you?
I guess it was the way I was living my life
We met in the midst of thugs
They introduced me to you
Ever since that day
Not even the President could tell me what to do
That feeling I got from letting go
I knew you could do damage
Damage is what you wanted
Damage is what you got
And on some of those nights
You were the reason I made it home
Now we are one
'Cause I live by, so I'll die by the gun
If I knew then what I know now
I would have left you alone

What They Are Missin'

By Antwon

I can look deep in any man's eyes
And see that the baby in him wanna cry
Because I am a young man full of wisdom and peace
Day by day God contains my inner beast
I'm tryna make sure that I stay away from darkness
Because where I'm from most people are dumbfounded and heartless
Trapped in a time of whips and hate
Going against the grain and killing their own race
Not knowin' where to look or how to find
Not thinking of the family the victim left behind
But in the streets you are forced to ride
The name of the game is "Do or Die"
They say you can take the man out the hood
But you can't take the hood out the man
And just like fools, we believe those words
Then have the nerve to wonder why we are caged up like birds
But it don't matter because we want the fame and fortune
With no responsibility
That's why our sisters are having abortions
I fear no evil as I give my mind time to grow
Not by the grace of man, but by the grace of God
I laugh in the face of danger, then feed those who starve
Not with chicken or ribs
But with history and faith
I guarantee people's stomachs
Will always feel that weight

CHANGE

Tha' Average Man
By David

What is life?
What does life mean?
It's more than cars and bling
Makin' it rain and serving fiends
We become mute
When someone speaks about Haile Selassie
Or the Prophet Marcus Garvey
But we know where the best clubs are at
Because that's where all the broads be
But we don't take time to hear the message
We treat it like a VHS tape
If the movie's dumb, we eject it
Now tell me if this is right or wrong
We can spit the hottest verse of a rap song
But can't do the same with the first Psalm
Man, I feel dumb
This ain't life

Change-like Symptoms
By Lonte

I refuse to stay in park
And become rusty and old
I want my value to go up
So I'll always be worth bein' sold
You can be stubborn and stay the same
But I'ma make a quick change
Like a Lambo switching lanes
Tryna get to its destination
One thing people fail to do
Is make change—a revelation
Well I'ma make an upgrade
While you clowns stay in clown stage
I'm glad unique sticks to me like glue
I'm daring to be different
I'm feeling sick with change-like symptoms

Waiting for Change
By Jermaine

Whether walking or driving or taking the train
This day to day sight, it's always the same
They beg or they fuss with their cup and a game
Outside of the train station waiting for change
Even in 90-degree weather or days full of rain
They'll stand on that sidewalk
Waiting for change
I once told a beggar, "Instead of complain
Pick yourself up, and get in the game"
So it's time to be brave and look life in the eye
Not wallow in sorrow and watch life pass you by
For a penny, a nickel or waiting for dimes
There's so much more to life
But we're wasting our time
There's so much to give and so much to gain
If we're not at the airport on time
We might miss our plane
Our flight to new heights and a new life to claim
Motivation to do is on you to attain
We can look through the window
And see the past in the pane
But can't look at ourselves and see we have to change
You might say it's crazy, I think it's insane
That we use everything except for our brain
Time to get off this road and make a new lane
Not stay like the guy on the sidewalk
Waiting for change

Change Comes
By Derrick

Change comes when you're sick and tired of being sick and tired
Or when your angriness expires
But until then
You're just a jail bug stuck in a bullpen
Waiting on the judge to seal your fate

Or the Marshal to lose the keys that open up the gate
Freedom, that's a lovely thing to people that don't have it
But people who do, take it for granted
It's easy to say you're going to change but hard to do it
Because how can you change if you're clueless
Maybe I'm just foolish
Could be I'm street influenced
Maybe if I was raised around the powerful and rich
My life wouldn't be full of could-haves and ifs
Maybe my whole meaning of being is a waste
My life is a 100% alcoholic beverage unchased
Sometimes I wonder if I was meant to be on this earth
Was I blessed with a gift or a curse?
Have I changed for better or for worse?

Moving Ahead With Excellence
By RaShawn

Coming from a messed up background where
Boys want to let off shots and lay strips down
Selling cocaine that is breaking our brothers and sisters down
So many near death experiences
I'm scared of death now
I been taught as a wild child
Never to back down
To walk with a smile
Though it should be a frown
Even when I was in school
Too busy trying to be class clown
Having long talks with my mom
She's praying that changes come now
It's a shame that I had to get locked up
To learn that only I can change my life around
Moving ahead with excellence is my motivation
Every time it gets hard
I just think of that phrase
And continue my education
Thinking about when I get my high school diploma
How much paper I will be making
When I have a family

Chapter 10

I will be bringing in all the bacon
I left bad and went good—no traces
Going to class in jail
Working ahead, no faking
These tests are my life
No time for procrastinating
School is the way I be raking in all the information
Instead of getting paid with money
I'm getting paid with education

Make Me Different

By Derrick

Make me different
So I can understand myself more
Make me different
So I can see me rich and not poor
Make me different
So the world can feel me
Make me different
So in the future my heart won't bleed
Make me different
So my seed won't see these same troubles
Make me different
So my life is not in a cage or a bubble
Make me different
So the world can see my talent
Make me different
Cuz street life and hope are unevenly balanced
Make me different
So I can finally say
"I made it!!"

CHAPTER 11

A BETTER WEAPON

A Better Weapon
By Andre

A poem is a better weapon
Than a knife
Because a poem will lead you
To a better future
To succeed
A poem will set your mind free
A knife will lead you
To violence
To jail
And maybe
To death

Listener
By Davon

There are things I can't tell my mother
So I come to you
I'll never tell my human friends
'Cause they don't listen as well as you
The way you listen
Is like a kid with his ear to a seashell
You hear everything I say
And the echo as well
I like the way you hold your water
And keep my secrets in your head
Paper, that's why you're the best listener
'Cause you never repeat what I said

Suited, Booted and Ready for School
By Major

I remember I used to get real fresh
I'd look like a young player
My mother used to make me wear a suit
Walking into school, at first I felt like a damned fool
I didn't know then how important I looked
In the classroom everyone thought
I was from a rich family
But I wasn't raised with a silver spoon
I was just suited, booted and ready for school

Pen Fiend
By DW

As I sit back
And operate this pen
I feel like I'm a pen fiend
Sick with words
Sick with the pen
Whoa! Just had a brain freeze
Right back at it
Like your everyday dope addict
Sick, can't go without it
Got to write about it
I see the light
And only I can see what to write
This is my life, I want to make it right
Some say pray to Christ
But every time I think about it
I am back writin' with the pen
Sick with so many emotions
And no one to talk to
Who can I turn to?
But my pen
I'm just your everyday pen fiend

My Free Mind

By William aka Prince Rich

My mind is now freed
On this pad I let my thoughts bleed
I don't have a one-track mind
I think of everything
My brain is racin' at lightnin' speed
I cried tears cuz I once was in need
I'm still physically locked up
But now my mind is freed
So at 10:45 when the door shuts
I pack my bags, and my mind takes me overseas
Then I'm somewhere on an island
Under them palm trees
I got a gift that we all need
A pencil, lined paper and eraser
So free ya' mind
You'll be surprised where it take ya'
I'm in my cell
But my mind 'bout to take me on a trip
I guess I'll see you later
When I'm back on the rip

I Bang the Poems
By Demetrius

I bang the poems for all problems
In all shapes, sizes and forms
I bang the poems for all weather
Cold, hot and sometimes warm
I bang the poems for the people
Who are looking for a sunny day
But can only find a storm
I bang the poems for the prison population
That's steadily growing
I bang the poems for the parents
Whose children get snatched off the streets
Without them even knowing
I bang the poems for all instruments
Tubas, drums and even French horns
I bang the poems for areas in poverty
Where every day guns are drawn
I bang the poems for my friend Dawann
Who died of a gunshot hole
In the same spot where his hat was worn
I bang the poems to death
From the day I was born

Scribbling In My Book of Life
By SN

My pain is like rain
It's drizzling on me
Soaked up with problems
I'm still lonely
My life feels like a book
With no words in it
It looks so bleak and empty
Maybe I should write on it

FREEDOM

Giraffe Neck
By Marc

Waiting for my release date is like
Climbing a giraffe's neck
So that's a long, long time
And it makes me stress
Seein' people leaving
Hoping my time is next
Getting tired of climbing this
Giraffe neck

Let it Ring
By DW

I sit back and wait
I ask myself, will she ever call?
So many days of stress and not being able to rest
Lets me know it's you I need in my life
Only you can fulfill my lust and happiness
I miss the way you smell, taste and feel...
It's like every time we meet
Something new always happens
And I find myself saying
Please, let it ring
It's been 26 months now
And I still can't get you back in my life
It kills me every day to see you pass by
I need you like life support
We belong together like day and night
But I just need you to do one thing
Let it ring
I open my eyes and see the sun shining in my cell window
I realize the wall is the only thing that separates us
It's eating me up like a worm in an apple
To know you're so close, but so far away
If there is a will or a way, can you please
Just let it ring?

If I Walked Out of Here Today
By Dimitri aka Black Moses

If I walked out of here today
I would probably pass out
Knowing I ain't gotta wear these jumpsuits
I would thank the Lord over and over for letting me be free
Letting me out of this coffin
This bathroom
If I walked out of here today
I would stand in the middle of the street
Just to smell the gas from the cars, trucks and buses
I would sit in the park around my way and just laugh
Knowing that I no longer have a certain amount of time to take a bath
If I walked out of here today
I would walk home
Just to get the feel of being free again
Knowing I can go to the one true place that I call home
If I walked out of here today
If I walked out of here today
If I walked out of here today
Damn! Let me stop thinking "If"
I just pray and wait for that day to come
When I'll finally be FREE!!

Free Mindz
By Michael

To have a Free Mind is to challenge all constraints
You have no complaints
You hold the key to your own freedom
There is no lock you cannot pick
There is no situation you cannot switch
There is no burden you cannot lift
Because your mind is meant to be opened
Like a given gift...

I Used To
By DC

I used to hold my head up high
Until the comments from C.O.'s
And big words from courtrooms
Knocked me down
I used to see the beauty in the sky
Until the horrific and bloody scenery
Stained my eyes from looking around
I used to live life without a care
Until I saw peoples' feelings get hurt with just a stare
Missing the times when I could feel happy
Without caution… yeah, I used to be free
I used to take things for granted
Now I miss and long for everything I had
I used to do what I wanted, didn't need luck
Can't wait for my next poem when I'll write…
"I used to be locked up"

HOME SWEET HOME

My Way Home
By DeVonte

Waiting for someone to find me
All alone with no one beside me
I'm stuck with a broken compass
And an intoxicated mind
I can't tell right from left, up from down
I been placed in the lost and found
But one day a caring heart
Came to show me my way
Fixed my broken compass
Detoxed my mind
And showed me my way home

Home Sweet Home
By Tavon

Home sweet home
I can just taste it…
Home sweet home
I'm racing for it…
Home sweet home
When I can just sit and have family time…
Home sweet home
I miss taking care of what's mine…
Home sweet home
I feel it…
Leaving this facility it's almost my time…
Home sweet home
I have a feeling …
So I'ma keep saying the line
Home sweet home
Home sweet home

WHO'S THERE?

Who's There?
By DeVonte

Who's there?
Who sees?
A lot of strangers judging me
Knocking and banging
But no one replies
Just birds singing
When I have questions
No one answers
I ask, "Who's there?"
But just see some stranger
He don't talk, he don't grin
Now I'm beseeching
For an answer again
Who's there?
Who's listening?
It echoes
Is my life a big collision?
Don't know but I wonder
Where will I go
When I'm six feet under?

What Happens When We Die?
By Major

What happens when we die?
Is it an everlasting burning fall?
Or is there really a heaven for all?
Is it lost souls
When the gates close?
What if I have good
That outnumbers the bad
But only by one good deed
Do I burn, or do I dance?

Make Me A Believer
By D'Angelo

If you can be around negativity
And still remain positive
If you can set aside your childish ways
And take responsibility for what you do
If you can have fear and faith in Allah
If wherever you go
You can show only your best
If you can worship without doubt
Have patience
And be steadfast in prayer
If you wish for your brother
As you do for yourself
You'll be a believer

Song From A Caged Bird

By Jonas

I'm a caged bird, eager to spread my wings
Ready to grace the world with such a beautiful thing
It seems my hopes and desires are simply dying
God gave me wings for a reason
I'm supposed to be flying
Flying high above the sky with the falcons and the eagles
Dapper in my brilliant attire, so naturally regal
Exploring different corners and climates of this beautiful land
Where we ran with the message of "Yes, we can!"
Yes, I am a creation of the God supreme
He gives us permission and power
To reach our goals and chase our dreams
And learn as we reap what we sow
And with every accomplishment
My wings will continue to grow
With the wind as my friend
I'm ready to begin a new journey, a new flight
Pushing the envelope for new struggles and new sights
Just letting my star shine
Giving the glory to God
Because without Him, I would be left behind
My faith will carry me in this time of trouble and stressing
I'm destined to be an eagle
Soaring with God's blessings

THE WORLD AROUND ME...

The Streets Are On Fire
By Christopher

The streets are on fire
Time to call a code red
Because 7% of my brothers
Are walking around with a disease
That makes me consider them the living dead
To have an expiration date, man, that's tough
When all this could have been prevented
If he would have wrapped it up

The streets are on fire
Time to call a code red
Because 3% of my sisters
Are walking around with a disease
That makes me consider them the living dead
To have an expiration date, man, that's tough
When all this could have been prevented
If she said, "Not unless you wrap it up"

The streets are on fire
Time to call a code red
When Washington, DC is not even a state
But we have the highest HIV/AIDS rate
Our streets are on fire
But there's something you can do to help
Put the blaze out
Start by being smart
And protecting yourself

Wrap it up!

Struggle of a Young Black Man

By Dimitri aka Black Moses

Hard times make me wish for the best
Being stereotyped as a black man
Still hasn't been put to rest
White people grab their purses and pearls
Because of my flesh
My skin is dark as the night
Not light and bright as the rest
I'm growing up in a single parent home
Constant gunshots at night
Start to bring aches to my dome
People killing my friends
Because they don't live on the same street
Now every time I go outside
On my waste is where I tuck my heat
The struggle of a black man
Started many years ago
But trust and believe
We got plenty more to go
If Martin Luther King didn't die that day
I probably would have more dreams at night
For my life today

Haiti

By John

Why Haiti out of all places?
I hurt when I see their eyes
I feel bad when I see their faces
The earthquake took more than a thousand lives
The government has enough money
But they don't mind when poor blacks die
I cried when I seen a dead baby
My prayers are with Haiti

The Infection
By Nick

The infection has spread like a disease in the air
Now here we are struggling and suffering
With this blindness and loss of intellect
The disease of retaliation
Has become our best friend
Living in the most unconscious places inside of us
The disaster of our infection plays out in many ways
Revenge, violence and death are contagious
Our untapped knowledge, wisdom and understanding
Is so powerful it could light up the Empire State Building
If we can just plug into it
We don't have forever
The disease will only get worse

Homeless Rhyme
By Anthony & Tyrone

Yeah, I'm homeless
With no chance of success
So I put my cardboard box
Down in an alley to rest
I have a cup
And a sign with a plea
But when people come by
They just laugh at me
They treat me like nothing
And act so rude
The only thing my belly can do
Is think about food
One thing I know
The shelter is on my side
They send me to a room
So I have a place to hide
Now I have hot water
And a sandwich to eat
A warm blanket and no box
Is better than the streets

Now I can sit back
And watch the hands of time
And think about my words
My homeless rhyme
One day I'll have big money n' big grips
Then I can be the one
To throw the homeless guys their tips!

Can You Explain To Me, Why?
By Andrew

Can you explain to me why
Life is so hard?
And explain why
Slim is a changed man, but can't get no job?
Please explain why
You can have fun one day and die the next night?
Can you explain to me why
Drugs are all over town?
And explain why
We come to jail and we get beat down?
Can you explain to me why
A girl was promised college, but she got slain?
Explain why
They won't put more cops on the streets, so the world can change?
Can you explain to me why
Lil' girls having sex for money?
Explain why
Slim is laughing?
But this is life
And I don't find nothing funny

CHAPTER 16

REDEMPTION SONG

Regrets
By David

The time that I've wasted is my biggest regret
Spent in these places I will never forget
Just sitting and thinking about the things that I've done
The crying, the laughing, the hurt and the fun
Now it's just me and my hard driven guilt
Behind a wall of emptiness I allowed to be built
I'm trapped in my body just waiting to run
Back to my youth with its laughter and fun
But the chase is over and there's no place to hide
Everything is gone, including my pride
I ask myself why and where I went wrong
I guess I was weak when I should have been strong
Living for the money and the wings I had grown
My feelings were lost, afraid to be shown
As I look at my past it's so easy to see
The fear that I had, afraid to be me
I'd pretend to be gangster, so fast and so cool
When I was actually lost like a blinded fool
I'm getting too old for this tiresome game
Of acting real hard with no sense of shame
It's time that I change and get on with my life
Fulfilling my dreams for a family and wife
What my future will hold, I really don't know
But the years that I've wasted are starting to show
I hope I can make it, I at least have to try
Because I'm heading toward death
And I don't want to die

The Guilt of the Hands
By Harold

People might not understand
But it's time for me to be my own man
My life is passing me by

But I did it with my own hands
I'm willing to accept all of the consequences
Because I have to let my hands
Speak louder than words
Seeing the pain in my mother's eyes
My actions with my own hands
Have given her a cold feelin'
That she sure doesn't deserve
My hands are filled with the most self-hatred
Resenting the objects they've become
The guilt keeps me humble
Because I understand what is done is done
In my hands, I'm looking for a change
But my vision is consumed by all the scars
With these hands I pray to the most gracious
Hoping that he frees me from these mental bars

How Has Jail Changed My Life?
By Doug

They ask me, how has jail changed my life?
Sounds like a trick question to me
'Cause so much has happened and it's not all bad
Since starting this journey I've lost eight friends I considered family
Some to the grave and some to sentences of more time than I can count
Don't get me wrong—most who are incarcerated need a time out
To see that the life they are living is a one-way street
I'm 19 and was part of that group
But now I realize I'm capable of so much more
For some reason, I was scared to succeed
Hard to admit it took these measures to help me see
That my strengths were in school
Not robbing or carjacking
It wasn't jail, but the people I met here
And the people who never gave up on me
Change started when I found a way to express myself
Thanks to Free Minds I now write poems
I fill my free time with reading
Instead of dwelling on my negative past
Jail isn't the safest place to grow up

But for me it was the best
It has molded me into the stand-up person I am now
And at the same time put my life on pause
But for some reason they keep asking me
How has jail changed my life?
It's still a trick question

Da Realest
By Jermaine

Dis is one of my realest poems eva'
I'm writing wit' dis pad
You can't win in the present
If you fightin' wit' yo' past
So just chill
Cuz if you reach, then freedom's in yo' grasp
Just tighten up dat grip
Whenever life is moving fast
Cuz when you don't dat's when you go down
I remember the times I was right there
Smokin' buds tryna get a buzz no light year
Yeah, dat lifestyle hardly bothered me
'Til I got behind bars charged wit' a gun and some robberies
Damn, not yet a man but in adult jail under Title 16
And being 16 made it hard to sleep
Thinkin 'bout all the things I was doing wrong
And everyone that doubted me
I swore dat I would prove 'em wrong
You gotta learn to never doubt ya' self
And never turn ya' back on Free Minds
They just out to help
When nobody else would
But if you ain't gonna help ya 'self
Then nobody else should
Half of my mans still in
So believe me I feel ya' pain too
The bigger picture is in plain view
Change wit' da time
But don't let da time change you

My Society's Problem
By Rapheal

People don't realize they have learned how to hate
It's so deeply embedded blocked by anger and fate
Friends pretend that they love the great life
But the truth of the situation is struggle and strife
Just like me, they have too much pride
But some don't have a struggling mom by their side
You see someone doing better
You rob him with no hesitation
You see hustlers with a quick solution
So you sell drugs to handle problems that's polluting
Hustling and selling gets you everything you need
But you'll always be incarcerated
Believe that indeed
People don't care who gets hurt
As long as they get paid by selling their work
Most don't have time to think about the police or dying
Feeling like they're already dead, their parents are left crying
I have pride in my culture and I know my heritage
I'm not worthless and I feel my advantage
The projects are designed for us to fail
We don't see the experiment living as young black males
You see, hate is a very strong word to a young man like me
But if you don't resolve the problem
Hate's consequences will last an eternity

Weight
By Donald

Weight under my eyes
Because I want to cry
Weight on my hands
Because I'm trying to push people to do good
Weight on my head
Because I'm learning so much
It's like I'm getting fed on Thanksgiving's weight
So much weight
I don't want to go back
I want to go straight

Dear Society
By Talib

Dear Society,

If you fear walking the streets for the crime I've committed
With all my heart, I'm sorry
I've learned my lesson through my incarceration
Now you don't have to worry
When I changed my thoughts, I changed my life
And now I'm looking back at my crime
I realize it wasn't right
Now I understand
You can still be accepted for doing positive things
You can do true work
Instead of plots and schemes
As I grow older I want to increase the peace
Put away the guns and squash all the beefs
I want to bring us together as one
Not worry about who you know and where you from
We can uplift the women
And be role models for the children
Just putting forth the effort
Is the way to begin

The Forgiveness
By Steven

I forgive my dad for walking out on his only son
I forgive the people who think they get over
When they assume that I'm dumb
I forgive life for dealing me this hand
I forgive my inner boy for not becoming a man
I forgive the man who bumped me
Because he couldn't see
I forgive...
But I can't forgive everything
Because I've yet to forgive me...

Rainy Days
By Alvin

A rainy day is the best day to me
Because it's peaceful, relaxing and it waters the crops for us to eat
On that type of day, I seem to sleep so well
I enjoy every bit of it because people can't get that down in hell
I like the way the clouds be thick and dark gray
Many people run for shelter, but I choose to stay
Right in the midst of it and let it shower down on my face
I look to the heavens and thank God for all his grace
I came to like the rain when I was eight or nine
My late aunt used to gather my cousins and I
We used to sit on the porch and each one tell a story
And when we would see lightning and hear thunder
She would tell us not to worry
I used to hear people say it rains because God is crying
So I guess God is happy when the sun is shining
I think it rains because the earth needs cleaning
But whatever the reason, I like the aftermath
When the rainbow be gleaming

Used To Be

By Gary

I used to be that person
That would stand on the corner selling drugs
Trying to keep up with the Joneses
I used to be that person
That would do anything to survive
In that jungle out there called the streets
I used to be that person
That was going to end up dead
'Cause I didn't know any better
I used to be

But now I am
That person that's willing to make a change
That person that's finally opened up his eyes
And seen that I have something to live for
That now I have another way out
I used to be a boy but now I'm a man
A man with goals
And a man that plans to live
And not to ever become
That used to be person again

UNSPOKEN WORDS

Heart and Eyes
By Lonte

I cover my internal bleeding with a smile
I feel non-human
Not cryin' in a while
I hurt, so why won't these tears fall over?
Maybe I cried enough for a lifetime
I'm becomin' mentally strong
I take blows from life and move on
I'd rather get over it then let life pass me by
Since life does not stop just 'cause I cry
I feel as if my heart and eyes never come in touch
Like they're beefing
And my heart says to my eyes
I'm leaving
Because we lost our connection
And I'm not receiving

The Vault
By DC

Locked away deep down inside
Is where my treasure lies
And my secrets hide
So dear and sacred to me it needs two locks
Not even the most sneaky could pick pock
My feelings collect dust, way down there
Just so I won't let 'em show out here
The code to the vault is truth
But I'm scared to unlock it
I wish my feelings, pain, and thoughts inside it
Could take off in a rocket
But they can't, so my secret storage will have to do
That's how I deal with things, how 'bout you?
When I have bad things happen or bad thoughts
It all goes in the vault

The Unspoken Words
By DW

I cry in silence
But the tears of my pen drip endless poetry
So many nightmares of untold war stories
The unspoken words of an accused young felon
Lost, confused, ignored and hidden
Redemption? No one seems to see the struggle
I will not let mental slavery deprive me
Alone I wait: 3 years, 2 months and 13 days
Innocent, but guilty in society's eyes
All eyes on me, but blind to the facts
Rehabilitation is what we yell for
The system holds the keys
They don't want you to see
Or me to succeed
The unspoken words of Title 16
I was 16 with no summer job
They say it's a bad economy
Streets were my only option
No role model, lost my daddy to the pipe
So I write, with the tears of my pen
Crying in silence with no voice
And so I need you to voice
The unspoken words of an accused young felon

Inside Pain

By Joshua
Dedicated to my sister and me

We feel this everyday pain
That can only come from grief and shame
No one to come to our rescue, no one to help us out
We hold on tightly to fear and doubt
We don't see the beauty of what this life can bring
We're screaming for help to anyone that can hear
Let the people come to us and lend an ear
To the pleading cries of need and guilt that we feel
We just need some comfort so that we may heal
From our wounded soul and heart
We were not like this from the start
In the beginning we were filled
With tranquility and peace
'Til calamity overtook us and we began to decease
We are calling
We are falling
Away from the people of the living
To the people of the dead

Heart to Stone

By Jonas

So the day before yesterday was kinda crazy. This dude I've gotten cool with here in prison, his baby's mother got shot up the other night. Apparently she was sitting in a car in front of her apartment building. She was shot twice in the head and once in the stomach.

My man was crushed. There's about five of us that kick it together, and all of us stayed outside with him until re-call, keeping him company and trying to comfort him. She's still alive, which is something, but that didn't keep my man from breaking down. Most of us were crying. I think it triggered some emotions in the others that they've been holding in.

Later that night while I was locked in my cell I did a lot of thinking about my man Debo. I was with him when he got killed back in 2002. I can remember a few days after he was killed, I was drunk, and out of the blue, I cried like a baby. Debo was too deep in a situation he couldn't get out of. Me and my cousin did a coupla' crazy things trying to help him, including breaking into this guy's house and taking every gun we could find, to try and slow him down a bit. But apparently that didn't help.

I can count on one hand how many times I've cried since then. Sometimes I question whether I've become emotionally detached. I can't remember the last time I had an actual argument with someone. Sometimes I just feel so indifferent, like it's whatever. I don't like it, but it's safe. It helps me stay sane. I recently ran across a quote from Oscar Wilde, he said: *The most terrible thing about* [prison life] *is not that it breaks one's heart—hearts are made to be broken—but that it turns one's heart to stone.* It was kinda' scary to realize how close to home that struck.

Anyway, it is what it is.

My Fugacious Life
By JohnQuan

fu·ga·cious   [fyoo-gey-shuhs]
—adjective
1. fleeting; transitory: 2. falling or fading early.

They want to know about my life
But why should I tell?
It's not like it's special or something
Just upsets and hell
Thinking I fell, never will prevail
Just doing time, alone in my cell
See, I like to write things
Hoping they change
But no matter how hard I try
The result is the same
Nothing but shame
To most it's cool
Just like a game
Stuck to my chain
Heart filled with pain
See that I know
Freedom must go
My fugacious life

JohnQuan was killed on August 14, 2008. This poem was read at his funeral.

Spoken But Not Heard

By Kenneth

From the pallid walls my voice emanates
It elucidates our struggle
It depicts frustration and rage
From when our voices were muffled
When no one listened or cared
Feelings were never spared
So hearts resembled prunes
Violence ensued
Leaving too many cold and blue
Blood-red tears cascaded
Down the cheeks of Mama's face
She cried as she consoled her baby
With her last loving embrace
Spoken but not heard!
Our cry for help rejected
Learning facilities neglected
Hearts dejected
By circumstance, nobody saw our anger
Danger followed
Murder hollowed bodies because they failed to listen
Intentions misunderstood due to malignant intuition
Sentences issued, toy soldiers locked away to decay from the inside out
Doubt filled our world with drought
Certainty never came
Red rain beating the roof of a house
Where grief and pain reside
Memorials raised
Pictures depicting fertile thoughts that strayed, then died
All we ever heard from the public was, Why?
Debating facts and fantasy as our worlds collide
Spoken but not heard

Gracias

Por Luís

Le estoy agradecido a todos los que han ayudado
Y las gracias no les he dado
Le estoy agradecido a los que me han dado la mano
Y ahora no los tengo de mi lado
Le estoy agradecido a los que me han hecho sonreír
Le estoy agradecido a los que me han dado animo para seguir
Le estoy agradecido a los que me ayudaron a caer bajo
Por que sin la ayuda de ellos
Nunca me hubiera levantado
Gracias a todos los que en algún punto de mi vida
Estuvieron a mi lado

Giving Thanks

By Luís

I am grateful to all those who have helped
And to whom I have not given thanks
I am grateful to those who have given me their hand
Though now they are not by my side
I am grateful to those who have made me smile
I am grateful to those who have given me encouragement to continue
I am grateful to those who helped me to fall low
Because without their help
I would never have gotten up
Thank you to everyone who at one point in my life
Was at my side

NOTE FROM THE EXECUTIVE DIRECTOR

Free Minds is based on a simple premise: books and creative writing change lives. In the nine years since we gathered for our first book club session in the DC jail's chapel, we have continually seen this truth played out. Free Minds members once resigned to a fate of prison or death on the streets, now find the inner strength to change. "Before I joined Free Minds I thought I was made for the streets and nothing else," says Delonte. "But they got me to write my first poems and read books. They helped open my eyes to bigger dreams and goals."

Books and poetry are only tools, though. Their true power is in the connections they foster. First, they can connect each of us to our inner self to help us discover our identity. "Books put me in a different state of mind to the point where I can dream that I am the character I am reading about," D'Angelo writes. Through biographies like <u>Makes Me Wanna Holler</u>, or <u>Always Running</u>, D'Angelo can imagine himself to be like Nathan McCall or Luis Rodriguez, both men who not only survived the streets and incarceration, but also transformed their own lives. Books and writing allow us to see who we are and what we might become.

As our members come to know themselves better, they want to share their experiences with those closest to them, creating stronger ties with family and friends. "I have seen things no child should see," Alonzo writes of his childhood. Parents, social workers and attorneys often tell us their surprise at the emotional openness Free Minds members express through their poetry. Writing is a safe space for young men to access and share feelings hard to speak face to face. Through self-expression and sharing, healing begins.

Finally, the written word creates connections with the wider community. Connections that bring youth hope, vital opportunities and a belief in themselves. It allows them to give back to the community and to repair some of the harm they have caused. By reading this book, you give each poet the gift of your support. Thank you for hearing their voices.

— Tara Libert,
Co-founder, Executive Director, Free Minds Book Club & Writing Workshop

Since its initial publication in 2011, *They Call Me 299-359* has provided a powerful tool for Free Minds to use in our violence prevention initiative, On the Same Page. Events are led by Poet Ambassadors—Free Minds members who have served their sentences and are back home in the community. The book allows them to engage with diverse audiences on issues of violence and incarceration and to find healing through the potent medium of creative writing.

Poet Ambassadors Shannon and Terrell have shared the book at gatherings from Washington, DC to Long Beach, California. They have read aloud and discussed poems by their incarcerated peers with everyone from executives at Google and professional consultants at Booz Allen Hamilton to public school children and Harvard Law School students.

"Sharing this book builds bridges between very different communities, bringing us all together, allowing us to see each other in a new light. Every poem that I've read from this book has affected someone. I've seen it with my own eyes— people gaining a new perspective, and understanding the mindset of someone who is different from who they are. I've met so many people in the community through this book that I never would have come into contact with otherwise. And the people on the outside, they want to know, they want to understand. The interaction is so important because it open everyone's eyes to what's happening in the community, which belongs to all of us. We are interconnected, that's a fact, and I feel a responsibility to work together to create greater understanding."

— Shannon, Free Minds Poet Ambassador

"When people read the poems in this book, they respond with love. It's always all love! Because reading another person's poetry almost gives you a superpower. So as a person on the outside, you might think, yeah, he's been locked up, or he looks and dresses a certain way, and might automatically reject that person. But then if you read his poems, you suddenly have an understanding of who he really is and how he is thinking. You see that he's smart and capable. And that helps the writer see the truth—that he is smart and capable. Poetry breaks down barriers. It allows us to see the whole person. And seeing one another's humanity makes us all more comfortable rubbing shoulders together!

"Taking this book into the community makes me feel so good. It's helped me to get over what I experienced. I was only 16 years old when I was first incarcerated and I spent 6 years behind bars. At first when I came home, I couldn't think about anything else but prison. Helping to educate others by reading and discussing the poems in this book? That's been an enormous part of the healing process for me."

— Terrell, Free Minds Poet Ambassador

BOOK CLUB & WRITING WORKSHOP

Empowering young inmates to write new chapters in their lives.

Free Minds Book Club & Writing Workshop uses the literary arts, workforce development, and violence prevention to connect incarcerated and formerly incarcerated youths and adults to their voices, their purpose, and the wider community. Since its founding in 2002, Free Minds has served over 1,500 individuals.

Free Minds' community of support engages members through four phases:

- Jail Book Club: Book clubs and writing workshops at the DC Jail and juvenile detention center, providing therapeutic group sessions where members participate in reading, book discussions, and creative writing exercises. Free Minds recently expanded their services to cater to the unique and underserved needs of incarcerated Spanish-speakers with the Mentes Libres ("Free Minds" in Spanish) Book Club and incarcerated women with the Women's Book Club.

- Prison Book Club: Free Minds provides crucial support to members incarcerated in federal prisons across the country due to DC's non-state status. Free Minds maintains long-distance correspondence by sending books, letters, postcards, the bi-monthly *Connect* publication, and encouraging feedback on members' poetry.

- Reentry Book Club: Free Minds supports members returning home through a job readiness and personal skill building apprenticeship, connections to job and educational opportunities, weekly book discussions and writing workshops, and a positive peer support network of fellow Free Minds members.

- On the Same Page: Free Minds members home from prison connect with diverse audiences from the community through this violence prevention initiative. Our members visit schools, universities, juvenile detention facilities, and community groups as "Poet Ambassadors" to share their life experiences and poetry. Participants share their perspective on the root causes of, and solutions to youth incarceration—a dialogue that promotes healing and nonviolence. Free Minds also brings our members' poetry and personal stories to the community through Write Night events. Volunteers gather to read poetry, meet the Poet Ambassadors, and write feedback for the incarcerated poets.

Free Minds Book Club & Writing Workshop is a 501(c)(3) nonprofit organization. For more information or to make a tax-deductible donation, visit our website at https://freemindsbookclub.org/.

OTHER YOUNG ADULT TITLES FROM SHOUT MOUSE PRESS:

How to Grow Up Like Me, Ballou Story Project (2014)

Trinitoga: Stories of Life in a Roughed-Up, Tough-Love, No-Good Hood,
Beacon House (2014)

Our Lives Matter, Ballou Story Project (2015)

The Untold Story of the Real Me: Young Voices From Prison,
Free Minds Book Club (2016)

Humans of Ballou, Ballou Story Project (2016)

The Day Tajon Got Shot, Beacon House (2017)

Voces Sin Fronteras: Our Stories, Our Truths,
Latin American Youth Center (2018)

I Am the Night Sky: … & other reflections by Muslim American youth,
Next Wave Muslim Initiative (2019)

The Ballou We Know, Ballou Story Project (2019)

For the full catalog of Shout Mouse books, including illustrated
children's books, visit shoutmousepress.org.

For bulk orders, educator inquiries, and nonprofit discounts,
contact orders@shoutmousepress.org.

Books are also available through Amazon.com, select bookstores,
and select distributors, including Ingram and Follett.

CPSIA information can be obtained
at www.ICGtesting.com
Printed in the USA
BVHW062022030521
606358BV00011B/216